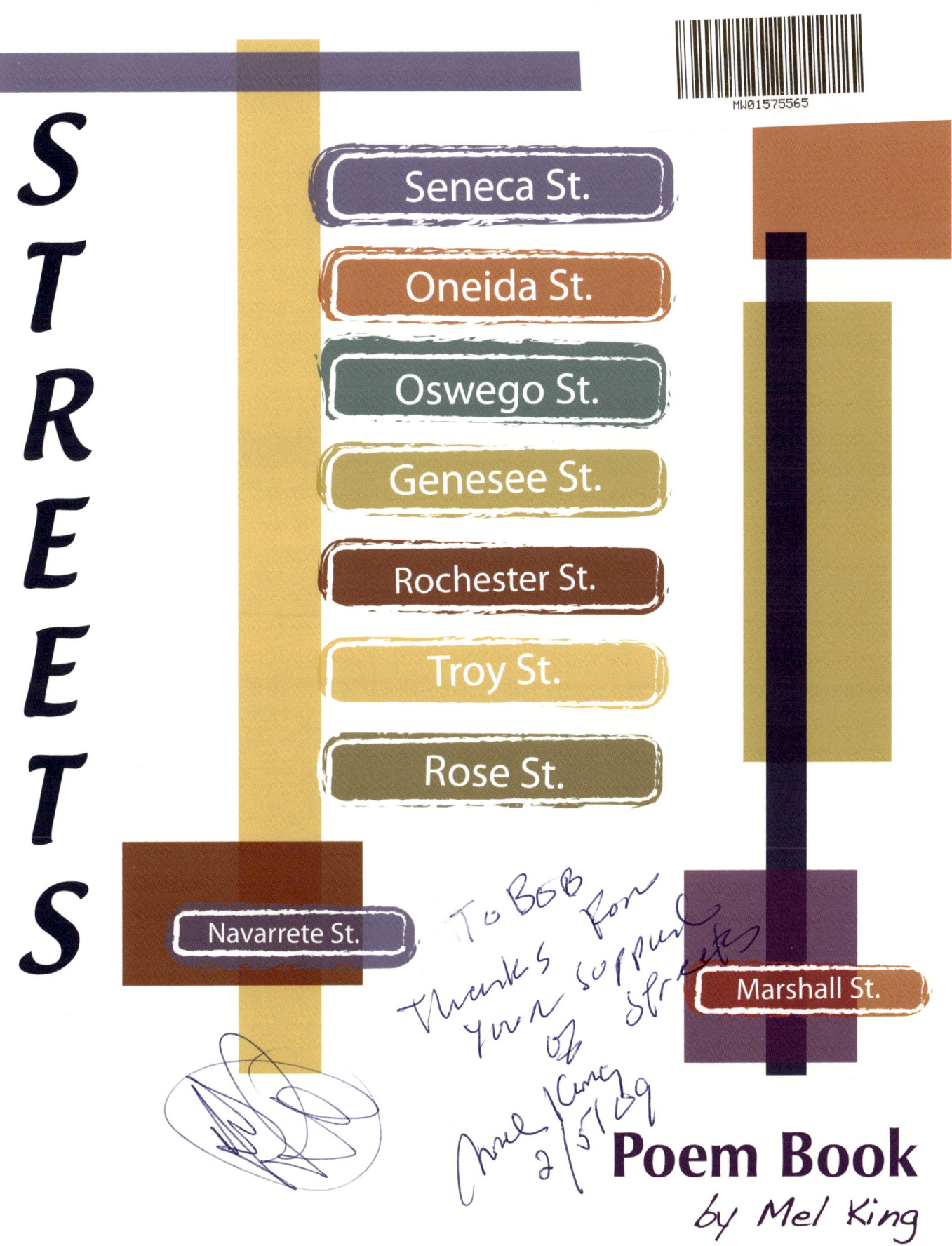

Streets, Mel King 1928

Copyright © 2006, Mel King. All Rights Reserved.

Published by Sensations Publishing
A Division of Sweetie's Books
Silver Spring, Maryland

http://sweetiesbooks.com/sensations.aspx

ISBN: 978-0-9820897-8-1

Cover and Interior Designers: Karen Spence and Susette Doran

Illustrations by Billy "Biz" Nunez, except "The Parade on Hammond Street" and "The Roller Skating Activity" by Allan Crite, and the fabric art wall hanging by Susan Thompson.

STREETS

INTRODUCTION

When asked "how long have you been working on this," the reply, "since 1928, when I was born" always gets a smile. It's the same answer I give when asked, "when did you get into politics?"

The first street I traveled was the one from my mother's womb; and my first political act was to cry for attention and get a response to my needs. This work about streets is about connections; a community reflection of the impact of the streets where I lived, and where the values that would lead me to learn to take the single "i" in live and shape it into a communal circle making it love.

The street where I was born no longer exists physically. Though urban renewal has claimed and eliminated it physically along with the other streets where I grew up, it has not erased the memories and impact of the extended family of people who came into my life from many parts of the world. I remember receiving the Traveler newspaper while at college. The headlines read that I lived in a slum, skid row. The shock and anger at the depiction of the area and the street that I called home was to be my first encounter with the process of devaluing a people so those with other interests would find it easier to take control. That issue, however, is for another time.

There are three struggles in life, those of the mind, the heart, and the land. Streets are land. It's what is in our hearts and minds that make the land have meaning, creating the basis for community. This idea was brought home in the year 2000 during a semester study through the International Honors Program when 30 college students studied life in three cities consisting of at least 10 million people making the neighborhoods of Cairo, Egypt; Mumbai, India; Rio and Curitiba, Brazil, our classrooms.

On the streets of those cities, the realities of living were played out each moment in the 24-hour day as work, family, community and survival intertwined. Here one learns the difference between the house, a physical structure, and a home, the caring relationships that bind people. The similarities in all these places were striking in that they were all struggling to maintain their land on the streets. A similar situation we witness here in the US is when city governments try to ban people in downtown areas who are without housing from engaging in activities that would help them to survive.

As I reflect on my street, and the ways in which people were included in all of the activities, it reminds me of verses in the book of Revelations that describe

Streets, Mel King 1928

a heavenly city where all the tribes are welcome. One example I remember vividly was the wedding party of two Armenian sisters that was held on our street so that all the neighbors could participate. All hands pitched in to sweep, scrub and wash the street so that the event could take place under the best of conditions.

During the summer evenings, all types of activities took place like boxing, singing and dancing to music played on a windup Victrola while showing people the latest jitterbug steps. Some of us would watch these scenes from our 2nd floor window wearing pajamas. And nothing deterred the older guys. When they wanted to play stickball, squash or two-hand tag, they cleaned the street even when it snowed.

As I grew older and was able to wander and wonder around the city, I became fascinated by the way the streets would take me and my imagination. One such example when walking with a friend, for what we thought was a good distance from our homes, was the time we found ourselves in front of the National Guard Armory on Arlington Street. As we looked in awe, it was obvious to us that raising the drawbridge over the moat area between the building and the street could block access to the armory. The purpose, we surmised, was to prevent those attacking from the outside from reaching those on the inside. Having been an avid reader of King Arthur and the Knights of the Round Table you can understand why this discovery had such an impact on a very inquiring mind. I remember saying to my friend that I wondered if Sir Lancelot had been there.

Recently a friend Robert Tannen remarked that "streets are public land, the most public property that belongs to everyone," so what we witness are folks who are the most attached to the streets for survival, constantly under attack by a variety of class and economic interests that fail to see them as human.

As a candidate for political office canvassing for votes door to door, and as a participant in parades, I developed a perspective about the uniqueness of different streets and avenues. In doing so, I found two things to be striking: the first was the different races, classes, and ethnic groups that would come out and stand at different points along the route. The second was seeing new shops and services established to serve a new population that had begun to move in. The multilingual signs on stores spoke to new ownership and an attempt to be inclusive. It didn't seem to matter which part of the city the parade was in; wherever I'd go, the patterns were remarkably the same. Which also made me wonder, where did the people who moved out go?

Streets, Mel King 1928

An answer may be that avenues created by mass transit's streetcars and trolleys took passengers out of congested cities to nearby suburbs. This phenomenon is well described in Sam Bass Warner's book Streetcar Suburbs. Mr. Warner traces how groups took advantage of the streetcars to form cultural communities in these new locations. We see the continuation of this practice with the development of the National Defense Highway System. This highway system provided access to cheap land and lower taxes coupled with easy credit to buy automobiles encouraging city folks to find housing and opportunities for employment outside of the city. It would also provide people an easy way to visit and enjoy this vast country. This system would eventually replace the railroad as a way to get goods and services to their destinations.

Streets come in lots of different forms and designations. They are called roads, lanes, pathways, boulevards, highways, turnpikes, cul-de-sacs, alleys, and routes. I like to think that railroads, rivers, canals, channels, tunnels, and bridges are streets; they are all linked and form a system like the arteries and veins in one's body. Like our veins, these arteries are used to circulate life-giving nutrients!

It is an easy stretch to see that streets are a vehicle for the key ingredients needed to maintain and sustain culture and growth. The real inspiration for this work is the humanity that binds the power of culture and the quest for life that is built on the power of love. I Identify culture as that which perpetuates one's family community group beyond survival to those actions and behaviors that lead to individual and community development.

Critical to this development is the exchange of ideas and ways of improving one's quality of life. Sometimes they come in material form such as minerals in foods, finery like The Silk Road from China, or spices from the spice route of Marco Polo. People have always strove to move from a position of struggle to a place that allows us to more fully develop.

Sometimes our rivers, railroads, highways, and turnpikes are seen as tools of development. The cost of building dams as sources of power and changing the course of rivers is expensive; however, no public expenditures match the sources used to build roads, streets and highways. For example, Boston's Big Dig is reported to be the single largest construction project ever built. Expenditure made so people and goods could more easily reach their destinations.

Streets, roads, highways, have also been symbols of political and social action as in "take it to the streets," and "take the high road" or in marches of the civil

Streets, Mel King 1928

rights movement, the picketing and boycotting that lifted Martin Luther King, the Greensboro students and in particular, Rosa Parks.

Roads are particularly connected to the economy; like housing, their construction is one way that economic growth is measured. But we also recognize the impact highways, streets, and the automobile have on health and the environment. And in far too many instances, armies have traveled roads in their efforts to build an empire.

It is said that all roads lead to Rome, yet one who brought a sense of salvation, celebration, and healing with open palms while building a movement based on the power of love did so on the road to Jerusalem.

The role that streets play in annual parades, appreciation memorials to veterans, or celebrating holidays, is also used to celebrate the home team that hadn't won a World Series in 80 years with a novel approach of a parade traveled by both land and sea.

Streets are a major player in all aspects of our lives. Just look at the many ways they shape our songs, poems and stories. There are over 50 songs and thousands of stories and poems inspired by roads and streets. Streets are also a part of our social rhetoric as in "street smart," or "hit the road, Jack!"

Inspiration for this work comes from several places. The first is all my friends, classmates, and family. I wouldn't have them if my parents hadn't made the voyage from Barbados and Guyana to North America, married in Nova Scotia then settled their way to the South End of Boston.

Another source of inspiration came from Joyce King who had persistently challenged me to right a wrong that occurred in commemoration of my 60th birthday. An oilcloth painting of the streets where we grew up was made without including her street. As a result, a page of this book includes Rose Street among the list of Indian Nation Streets.

As I was going through this process, there was always something lurking in my mind about streets. At some point it became evident that I had seen some of the work of Alan Crite's who, in the 1930s, had drawn paintings of activities on his streets. I kept remembering one of his paintings, which was about a parade on Hammond Street. Later in leafing through a book of his work I was amazed to see how in fact he had already done the work on streets in a far more imaginative and creative way. With all due respect and humility I like

Streets, Mel King 1928

to dedicate this Poem Book to Allan Crite, a chronicler of life on the streets of Lower Roxbury, whose works are an embodiment of the phrase "a picture is worth a thousand words."

I had the good fortune of being connected to and supportive of an incredible youth development program for the past 14 years, Artists For Humanity. I presented the members with this project and indicated that I wanted some illustrations in the book. Several weeks later, thanks to Claudia and Biz, they presented me with some illustrations they thought would fit. All except for "The Parade on Hammond Street", "The Roller Skating Activity" by Allan Crite, and the political poster by Susan Thompson, the illustrations are the work of Billy "Biz" Nuñez. Susette Ricardez Duran was in need of a project to do for her class at Bunker Hill Community College, so she created and implemented the design concept in what she describes as a Poem Book, and Karen Spence put the final touches on the design and layout. The result speaks for itself.

Streets Team: Billy "Biz" Nuñez, Susette Duran, Mel King, Karen Spence

Streets, Mel King 1928

Streets

From time to time you
have to live in
the Street.
I mean be alive in the
place that
is defined by you
Your presence even
for a minute
informs the Street
even though
the name
hasn't changed
it's not the same you
made it different
Young people on
bikes change it
and leave a memory
when they fall
Babies in strollers in
arms or on
shoulders know

Streets, Mel King 1928

From windows balconies and steps
are eyes that shaped the Street

as do the sun and
moon which shine
on the Street where
I live

This is my Street
and I must live my
life now in
this moment
as I put one foot in
front of the other
going where the
Street takes me or
my life

There are Streets of
hope that hide despair
some that rise others that fall
with flowers and trees

Streets, Mel King 1928

Hydrants for cooling

caverns for utilities sewers for drains

to flush the horse manure washed down

by the rain

Streets, Mel King 1928

Streets are for games like hopscotch

Streets, Mel King 1928

Stick ball

kick the can jump rope and dodge

Streets, Mel King 1928

Streets are symbols of living
Streets make connections to places
and people
uptown downtown crosstown to bridges are
bridges underground

Street is where we meet on the sunny side
under lampposts where lovers stroll

Streets, Mel King 1928

On some streets, there are no sidewalks

Others bricks cobblestones paved in concrete or asphalt
others with good intentions

Streets, Mel King 1928

Streets give you identity
make you real
for elections assistance an
address so you can
be found

Streets have expectations
make demands for
uniformity a way of living
visual visceral like
in Baltimore
where the steps are
painted the same
Streets identify
neighborhoods sometimes
neighbor hoods turf for
the young associations
for the
civic minded
organizers of block
watches flea markets
parties or fish fries

Artist: Susan Thompson

Streets, Mel King 1928

Rivers streets canals and channels are
Streets for barges and boats and
houses that float
where otis could sit on the dock of the bay
and watch the clouds sail by

Streets, Mel King 1928

Some streets have initiatives like Dudley
where building community power is shared

*Some steets have Corners
with memorials of lives
ended too soon*

Streets, Mel King 1928

Streets are where we celebrate Saints the Virgin and the Stations of the Cross

Streets, Mel King 1928

Streets are a haven
a host
A place to rest where
there's a house with
a light
and one can be safe

where you learn lessons
that shape your life

> **Impressions or how did you get that way**
>
> Sunday on Seneca street
> a trip to the store
> followed home
> by a man to the door
> quickly inside and slam
> in his face
> only to learn was not an
> act of good grace
> my fathers stern clear tones
> opens the door and
> welcome to our home
> you're hungry and cold
> we'll sit by the stove
> biscuits and beef
> raisin pie that is sweet
> are warmed while the tea
> from the stove provides
> the body with heat
> saw the child knew a
> family was near
> sorry my approach
> caused him fear
> been a long cold trek
> walking these dark
> and icy streets
> thanks to your kindness
> I can be on my way with a
> full stomach and toasty feet
> whatever you have was
> the lesson for me
> you always share with those
> In misery
> we never close doors to
> those in need ones heart
> never shut to those we can feed
> no matter what we have there is
> something to share
> the most important of course
> is that we care

Streets, Mel King 1928

Streets are where we share our arts and crafts

Streets are where we talk to our neighbors

and invite their support

Streets, Mel King 1928

Streets are everywhere you walk or run

Streets, Mel King 1928

Streets lead us to the Temple in the mountains when it snows.

Streets, Mel King 1928

Parade on Hammond Street, Allan Crite

Streets are where you watch a parade
where holiday symbols are displayed for sales
and a beat for drummers and police

Rue in France calle in Spain rua in Portugues
sometimes called paths or pathways avenues
or lanes
undiminished as alleys or roads
and embellished as boulevards or parkways

Streets, Mel King 1928

Linked as causeways underground and
water as tunnels
and hairpin turns around mountains
in the sunlight and moonbeams

Streets, Mel King 1928

Street have signs that help you to know where you are where you are not

on long trips from the back seats you hear are we there yet

we're bored are there any more games to play

Streets, Mel King 1928

Streets are where a plot of land gets attention

and its growth offers different views
some weeds edible and attractive
others are unplanned still natural and green
and flowers express a neighbors artistic bent
with colors bright to enhance the view

Streets, Mel King 1928

Memories of steps taken before

of visitors from other places

skid row in the cold
seeking shelter with a bottle on hip
sometimes shade from the heat of the sun
startled feet marking the quickest route
over pressed earth sometimes red
others brown and white when
covered with snow

Streets, Mel King 1928

With signs that say stop and go

or tell you when you can speed and when to go slow

Streets, Mel King 1928

You don't lead the Street

you follow where the Street leads you

Streets, Mel King 1928

Street is where you watch fireworks and perched on the bank's steps applauding the burst of light and colors the world comes to ooh and aah

in the common language of awe and delight

Streets, Mel King 1928

The words may differ, the meaning in the sound is the same

Streets, Mel King 1928

Street is where someone puts up a net and there is a volley of balls amid shrieks and yells for the ice cream cart's bells

Streets, Mel King 1928

Double dutch – and little Sally playing in the water
roller skates on boards forerunners of the skateboard

The Roller Skating Activity, Allan Crite

Ballooned tired bikes with coaster brakes
by Columbia and Schwinn
with a place for a favorite person to sit
Streets were alive in winter when it snowed
on flexible flyers down our hill we would go

Buck buck how many fingers have I got up
the call for choosing sides
as our model planes would rise off ground
or get launched from a window on the world

Streets, Mel King 1928

Streets have character
there's Basin and Bourbon the Streets of the blues
Fifth Avenue for bonnets and
new shoes for dancing all over heaven
Wall for financial news
At Xmas salvation arms for alms
Easter for the frills on the bonnet
Heart Break Hill in the Marathon
Nob as in cable cars
Sugar as in where you lived
where cows hoofed to graze in the commons
institution like church and school and
state as in Massachusetts
names Seneca Oneida Genesee Oswego Shawmut
give the Indian nations their due

Streets, Mel King 1928

Team mates Ambrosini Perella Maleonis Unwar Goldberg King developed their roots or was it the route of the rainbow

Streets, Mel King 1928

Formed in a coalition in a campaign for mayor

Streets, Mel King 1928

Some streets have numbers where you get your kicks like 66
and link Chicago and LA
others after kings like Charles some for flowers like Rose fruits
like Peach or nuts like Pine

Streets, Mel King 1928

There are streets that define water like Ocean and Beach spring river and lake where a picnic basket with goodies mom cooked potato salad fried chicken

And some streets where your family inflates a pool and you splash

Laugh at the heat from your neighborhood beach
Streets go round about circles called squares
when honoring those whose deeds we remember
while pausing for the four legged animals
who made the road before

Streets, Mel King 1928

There are coffee houses where the men hide
with water cooled hashish and tales of old
in the midst of dominoes backgammon chess checkers on

Benches while outside the dice roll against the curb or building wall

Streets are a venue for prostitutes and hustlers
hawkers and peddlers for rags and bottles
fresh fish get your Porgies today
matzos and 'ranges as the words faded away
some came with goodies like roasted chestnuts
and popcorn waffles melted butter lemon slush
and snow cones

Streets, Mel King 1928

Some Streets had all you needed
bakeries with pizza and cat pies
Pita bread bulkie rolls pasteles and pan de aqua

Streets, Mel King 1928

Groceries from everywhere

matzos kielbasa feta cheese rolled apricot sheets
delis with pickles and pastrami
pistachio and frozen pudding ice cream
candy with the cod liver oil from the drug store
eel for the holiday wine whiskey and beer
needle and thread for repair
Vaseline for skin and the hair
polish for the shoes

Streets, Mel King 1928

Streets were a stage for the organ grinder's monkey
to dance to
the accordion players tunes and
the band from South Carolina raised money for their school
on Streets like Peixto in Rio in summer
the music is cool

you stop listen watch

> Sidewalk shows
> Summer sounds
> Strings soft sweet
> Sticks strumming Savoring suds Singing songs
> Sharing stories Standing seeing Social society Sentiments searched
> Street scene
> Smiles of satisfaction Sensuous syncopation Slowly sheds
> Shields shells Sophisticated staccato Saluting senses

Streets, Mel King 1928

Some are named for places where we were born
Like Aguadilla or Plazas like Betances and San Juan

We paint murals to show life back home and
our presence here

Streets, Mel King 1928

Street is where the art of break dancing began
so you wouldn't have to fight to show you are better than
or draw the line in the sand

A lesson for all who would heed sharing one's gifts
can eliminate the weapons of destruction need
Street is where the turntable became an instrument of change
and gave the sounds of music a pulsating range as the
spoken word built on Baraka the Last Poets and Sanchez
un rapped Hip Hop and a cultural change that spread
across Streets everywhere

Streets, Mel King 1928

Streets are where we listened to orators for causes like
Malcolm and Martin Felix Angela Davis
the Turners Nat and Chuck

Joined marches for justice heard prayers for salvation

From afar they are paved with gold
And viewed as the Road to success
Street is where community begins
When all the tribes are welcome
Streets can lead to freedom and joy
overland where Paul rode the Road to sound the alarm

38

Streets, Mel King 1928

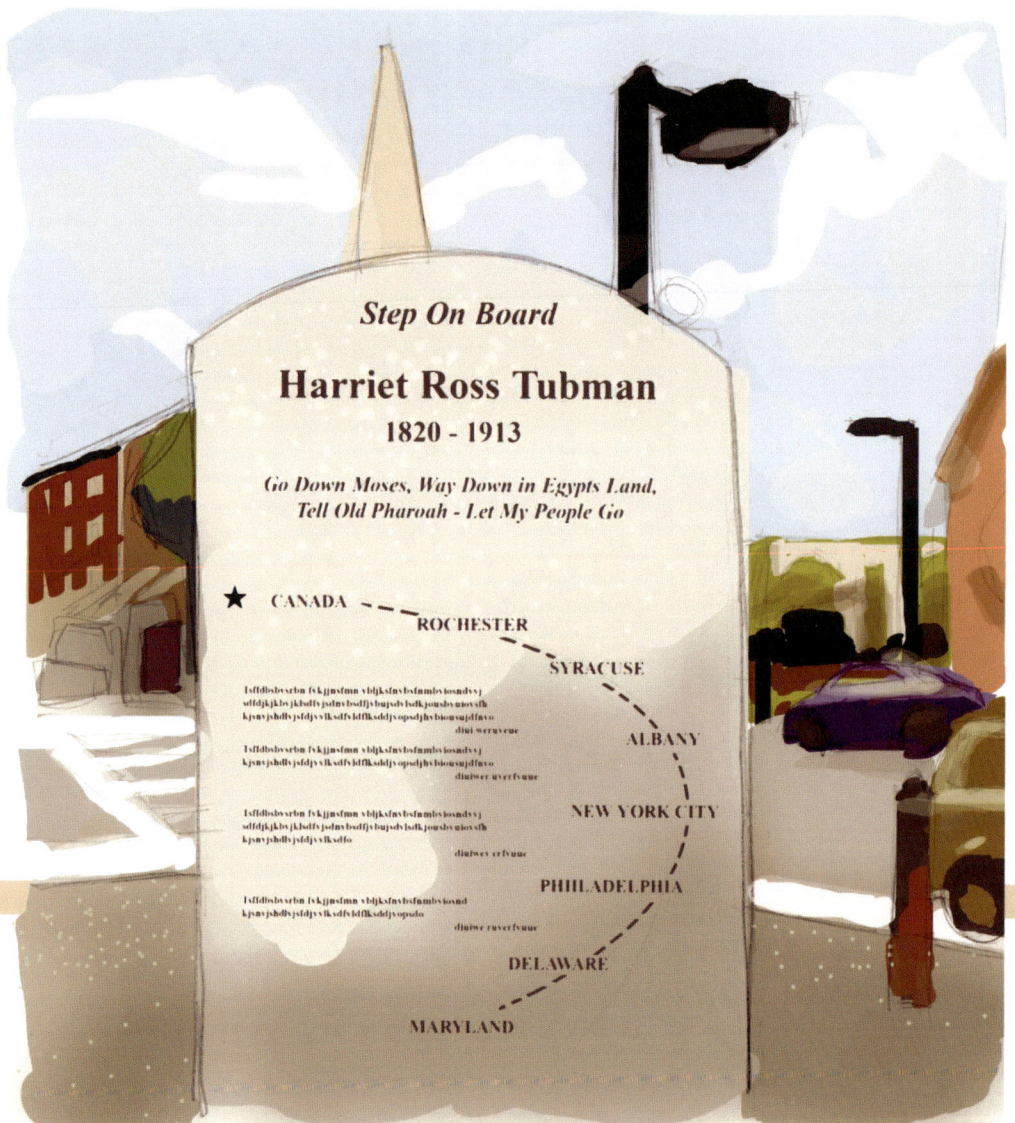

Or Harriet Tubman's underground route
where she rescued her people from slavery's harm
Streets provide the new arrival a place
to call home
where we gather together to give thanks for our blessings
knowing we have found the Street
of our dreams

Streets, Mel King 1928

Streets are metaphors where I have come to the
end of my road
Street smart and wise can look backward in time
Real as the stony Road we trod with our weary feet
"lifting every voice"

Symbolic in stories like Tobacco Road that give a snapshot of
some of our lives and where we abode

Putting gestures like one for the Road of course there are folks
who take the high Road
then there's the silk Road the merchants traveled to
peddle their wares
toll Roads and in fables where the troll collects his due
for the trucks like Ford built for the Road ahead

Streets, Mel King 1928

The public works to keep them moving with

   earth movers
        and Street pavers

Streets, Mel King 1928

Roads have signs that look out for the deer others like the billboard in Tennessee that shows you care and ways of expression like…

For a poet, Street is living by the side of the road so you can be a friend to all with a light that shines to show the way home.

Streets, Mel King 1928

List what you remember most from your street or neighborhood...

Streets, Mel King 1928

Draw Your Street

Printed in the United States
136320LV00002B